THE POWER OF PRAYER

THE HIDDEN POWER TO LISTENING TO GOD

Maria Reems

authorHOUSE®

AuthorHouse™
1663 Liberty Drive
Bloomington, IN 47403
www.authorhouse.com
Phone: 1 (800) 839-8640

Published by AuthorHouse 01/13/2017

ISBN: 978-1-5246-2541-2 (sc)
ISBN: 978-1-5246-2540-5 (e)

Library of Congress Control Number: 2016913552

Print information available on the last page.

This book is printed on acid-free paper.

ABOUT THE AUTHOR

Pastor Maria Reems is a wife, mother of three daughters, and copastor of the Center of Hope Community Church in Oakland, California, and she serves alongside her husband, Pastor Brondon Reems. She is an anointed dynamic speaker, preacher, and teacher. In addition, she is a professional consultant and has the added responsibility of providing services, including community relations training to nonprofit and for-profit organizations.

Pastor Maria is a strong advocate for women while promoting and utilizing spiritual healing as an empowerment tool, following in the footsteps of her mother in love, Bishop Ernestine Reems. She has founded and facilitates Women on the Move, a professional organization for women seeking to be empowered and transformed through life's journey. Since the year 2009, the organization has sponsored a free annual health and career fair for the entire city of Oakland.

As a former corporate executive and schoolteacher, she integrates her professional background and corporate experience to empower others to maximize their talents and abilities. She is an advocate for women and their healing and empowerment.

ABOUT THE BOOK

In April 2014, I decided to reach out to a wider community by writing an Internet blog so that I could share my thoughts and feelings about life, love, and my faith in the hope that it would offer some small amount of comfort and encouragement to others going through life's process. My blog has gone from strength to strength, and I have received many messages and kind words about how my website has helped both men and women, old and young, on their journey through life. My first e-book, When You Walk through a Storm, written in 2015, grew from that idea. It explained how faith in God can help you through the storms of life. Now, one year on, I feel the time is right to put pen to paper again. This time I want to talk to you about the power of prayer and how it can help you through the process of life. Prayer is an important part of my faith, and I hope that this little book can help to strengthen your own faith and bring you closer to God through the power of prayer.

DEDICATION PAGE

I would like to dedicate this book to two very Special Women in my life. My mom, Millie Lyons who is rejoicing in heaven since Dec. 2014. & my mom in love Bishop Ernestine Cleveland Reems.

You have been an Inspiration and an excellent example of Motherhood to me. I want to thank you for your unconditional love, your support & your prayers. Your labor was not in Vain!!

I want to thank you for your Prayers and love that you have demonstrated to me and the family. Because of your faith and your willingness to never give up, you have taught me to keep believing & maintain a consistent Prayer Life!!

Love you,

CONTENTS

THE POWER OF PRAYER

Ephesians 6:16-18 (ESV)
In all circumstances take up the shield of faith, with which you can extinguish all the flaming darts of the evil one; and take the helmet of salvation, and the sword of the Spirit, which is the word of God, praying at all times in the Spirit, with all prayer and

> supplication. To that end keep alert with all perseverance, making supplication for all the saints.

If someone were to ask me what is the common denominator in Marriage, Motherhood and Ministry my honest answer would always have to be – PRAYER! I would shout it from the rooftops.

There is such power in prayer. Theologians have written about it. Our leaders have spoken about it. And recently scientists and medical experts are finding that prayer really does work.

We must constantly pray for our marriages, our ministries, and most especially for our children.

But here is the important point. Prayer is about communication with God. Communication is a two way process. It is about talking, and then listening – listening to what He has to say in return.

> Matthew 7:24 (NIV)
> Therefore everyone who hears these words of mine and puts them into practice is like a wise man who built his house on the rock.

Sometimes it is easy to keep talking to someone about your problems, your dilemmas and mistakes. But that is just not enough. The Art of Prayer is in the Listening.

Have you mastered the ***Art of Listening***? Or are you just monopolizing the conversation?

Can we listen to God once we have spoken and made our shopping list of requests? We give Him a detailed list of what's not working, how we are feeling and what we think we need to be fixed in our lives. But then do we really listen to what He has to say in return?

I know this might seem harsh. Well, it's because I have been in that place where all my prayers were about me! I call it the 'What About Me Season"? Does anybody care how I feel? Is anyone listening?

Through prayer, I received a short but sweet answer that went something like this – YES, I MOST CERTAINLY DO!

MARIA, YOU SERVE A GREAT BIG GOD WITH GREAT BIG PLANS FOR YOUR LIFE AND IT IS MUCH BIGGER THAN YOU THINK!!

Now I understand.

THANK YOU GOD FOR THE POWER OF PRAYER!!

THIS THING CALLED FAITH AND MARRIAGE

Prayer can help you in many situations as you work your way through the process of life. One of the biggest events in your life will be when you marry. Loving and praying together will be the start of a lifetime of happiness together.

> Mark 10:6-9 (NIV)
> But at the beginning of creation God 'made them male and female. For this reason a man will leave his father and mother and be united to his wife, and the two will become one flesh. So they are no longer two, but one flesh. Therefore what God has joined together, let no one separate.

Recently, we celebrated twenty three years of marriage and looking back, I can see that my marriage has gone through the process. Some ups, some downs, some good, some bad but it was all in the process.

The more and more I think about life and life's lessons the more I tend to believe that life is a process. Esther in the bible had to go through a rigorous process in order to find favor with the king. She had to go through a Preparation Process!

In my own marriage raising three girls, attempting to balance school, extracurricular activities, friendships and church activities has been overwhelming at times.

Serving in the Ministry alongside my husband for approximately 10 years, I must admit has required commitment, dedication, time management and a whole lot of prayer! Prayer has allowed me to become the woman that I would never have thought possible. It has taught me patience, endurance and determination while allowing God to do extensive surgery on my heart.

Marriage is a lifelong commitment. According to Webster's dictionary it is the state of being united to a person in a relationship. I have found that I must constantly work and build on my relationship.

Date nights, worshipping together, open communication and intimacy are the by-products of a healthy relationship

There are times when I cannot see what God is doing in our Marriage but I must wait and believe by Faith that it will get better! God does not place a time limit on our waiting, he only requires that when we trust and believe, eventually it will come to pass.

> Hebrews 11:1 (KJV)
> Now, Faith is the substance of things hoped for, the evidence of things not seen.

The process of life is amazing. I have no regrets! If someone were to ask me if I could do it all over again, what would I do differently? I would honestly say, "Don't buck the process"

WHY PRAY FOR OUR CHILDREN?

Over the years your life will change. If you are blessed with children, prayer can be your comfort and your guide.

> Proverbs 22:6 (KJV)
> Train up a child in the way he should go: and when he is old, he will not depart from it.

How many times have you sent your children off to school, said 'goodbye' and noticed that something was not quite right and you just can't stop thinking about it.

All day long they are on your mind. You feel uncomfortable because you know you have left something undone. I must confess, I have experienced this many times, and I have learned from experience that when this happens, you should take action, ask questions, and most important of all – begin to pray for the children!

Prayer is an essential tool in our children's lives. Children are exposed at a young age to many negative forces: peer pressure, violence, drugs and alcohol are just a few. We need to counteract these negative forces and we can do this through prayer. It is important that we pray for our children every day.

As parents we all desire the best for our children. We want them to make the right choices so that they become productive citizens in society. However, if we do not model the discipline of prayer into our children's lives, how will they ever know the power of prayer?

Here are just a few reasons why we should pray for our children:

1. Children model themselves on what they see. When my children see me praying, when they are in need of prayer for a situation in their lives, they will approach me and ask me to pray with them.

2. Prayer has taught me to wait on God for direction, before attempting to solve the explosive situations in their lives.

3. Prayer will help you to love your children unconditionally, even if you do not always agree with them, and some of the choices they make during their life's journey.

As you can see, these are just a few reasons why we should pray for our children. There are many, many more.

For details of my CD, 'A Parent's Prayer' see:

http://www.mariareems.com/shop

TRIBUTE TO AN AGEING PARENT

Family life is not just about caring for your children. Life's process brings other heavy responsibilities too, but prayer can give you the strength to cope with anything.

Exodus 20:12 (ESV)
Honor your father and your mother, as the lord your God commanded you, that your days may be long, and that it may go well

> with you in the land that the lord your God is giving you.

A couple of years ago I took on the responsibility of taking care of an ageing parent whose health had taken a major downturn. We decided to put her home up for sale and move my mom into our home. And I also became responsible for all medical appointments and transportation. When I started out honestly, I did not know what this would entail.

It seemed like only yesterday she was a perfectly healthy 78 year old, independent, enjoying life and her retirement years with family and friends. I think I always knew deep down inside that one day this would happen, but honestly I never thought that I would be in this position, caring for an ageing parent, this soon. Now it seemed we had exchanged roles. I had become the parent and she the child.

However, I still had Mama. The one who took care of me while I was sick. Mama who made sure we had hot meals on the table each night. Mama who took care of our basic needs and would sacrifice her happiness to make sure we were provided for. Thank God for Mama!

Now, mama has her good days as well as bad days. Some days are better than others which makes my job that much harder. Wishing that the good days would far outweigh the bad ones.

Please don't misunderstand me. I am not complaining or regretting my decision to take care of my ageing parent. Matter of fact, I see this as an honor and a privilege to serve her in the way that I am able to. I see it as a way of repaying her for the many sacrifices she made over the years for me and my sisters, for us to be able to live a better life.

If you find yourself in this situation my advice to you would be

1. Ask for help.

It can all become overwhelming. I reached out for help, calling all family members, friends as well as my church family. And remember with God in your life, you are never alone.

2. Remain faithful to prayer

This is not the time to ignore your prayer time. Be determined to keep that prayer time you have established between you and God. Prayer will help and strengthen you to make wise decisions regarding your ageing parent as well as the rest of your own family.

My prayer for this season in my life is “Lord, allow me to give back all that my Mom has so blessed me with over the years”! I will not complain, be angry or bitter. Because it is truly a blessing in disguise to be able to give back to someone who laid down a sacrifice for you.

Thank you Mom for the gift of life and becoming a living example of unconditional love.

“All I want is to say is Thank you!!”

BROKEN BUT BLESSED

The power of prayer is not just for others. Sometimes you must ask for help from God for your own sake, and God is always there for you when you need Him most.

"Brokenness is for a season but the lessons from it are for a lifetime. Keep holding on."

Ps. 34:18 (NLT)
The Lord is close to the brokenhearted; he rescues those who are crushed in spirit.

Have you ever questioned your life and the problems and situations in it? When I was growing up I was the youngest of three sisters. It seemed to be that they were allowed to get away with everything and anything I wasn't that fortunate. Who could I seek to resolve this issue? I wasn't an extremely spiritual child, however, deep down I knew that GOD had a great purpose in my life and this experience was only a setback to allow God to heal my brokenness!

Life teaches us to despise brokenness. Broken things are worthless. Most of the time we go buy new and replace our broken things. We toss them. They are not worth the time and energy needed to repair the brokenness.

Unfortunately, we do the same thing with people. It just takes too much time and energy to repair them. Unconsciously, we toss them away. We are too busy and important to take broken lives into the repair shop of our heart and begin the work of repairing.

As I journeyed through my teenage years and young adult years, I was exposed to and curious about lots of things. My first real experience was over twenty years ago when I entered into an unhealthy relationship. Sure, I was still young and impressionable and it was always popular to be in a relationship to receive affection and attention from another person, but I believed that this was the "ONE", the one person whom I would spend the rest of my life with, and as unhealthy, painful, and dark and disappointing as it was, I was determined to stay in it, but for a while. My flesh believed that the pain I experienced in this relationship was alright, despite my fear, my sadness, and pain. I was broken and shattered, and, though I believed in a God who desired my healing, I wondered whether I would make it through the brokenness to a healed and whole self.

Broken (adj) = Subdued totally;
humbled: a broken spirit.

I struggled to get out of this thing that had become a situation rather than a relationship (in my mind), which was very challenging. This was one of the hardest struggles of my life. I looked for assistance from another person but to no avail. No one could help me with my exit. However, I was addressed with more pain: I was informed of the lies, the cheating and more disappointments and this made me feel even worse. At this point, I started to question God. “God, where are you?” If you are truly present why won’t you answer me?

I didn’t realize that God never left my side. The hole in my heart was for God to mend: through my tears and long nights I was still comforted. I continued to speak to God asking lots of questions and telling him all about my anger and my disappointments. God did answer. He wanted me to surrender and my healing could only happen through Him.

I had an epiphany. God desires healing in all of our lives, no matter what we go through and how hard it seems to get out of hard situations. God has a bigger plan for all of our lives, our will is not our own – it is God’s. I also recognized how patient God was with me, when I saw the clear signs to exit out of this relationship and other things that were not healthy for me, His love continued to cover me and guide me. If I would just be patient with Him and myself, the hole in my heart could be mended.

> Ps. 18:6 (NIV)
> In my distress I called to the Lord;
> I cried to my God for help.
> From his temple he heard my voice;
> my cry came before him, into his ears.

GROWING YOUR FAITH

The power of prayer can help your faith
in God to grow strong and true.

Rom. 10:17 (NASB)
So faith cometh from hearing, and hearing
through the word of God

Many books have been written on faith. There are many experts and sermons that discuss faith. However, growing your faith is an ongoing process that never ends. Faith is like a seed. When you plant it your faith will grow as long as you feed it. The big question is how do you grow strong in your faith so that you can be free from doubt and worry?

Here are my tips for growing your faith:

1. Feed your faith by reading the word of God.

There are many scriptures in the bible about faith. Each day try to read bible scriptures that will build your faith.

2. Exercise your faith

Just like you exercise your body, you must exercise your faith.

3. Free your faith from negativity

Stay away from negative people. You must feed your faith and not your doubts,

4. Share your faith with others

It is important to share your beliefs with others so that they may hear it and may remind you at times of what you professed.

5. Spend time in prayer

This last is the most important of all. Take some time out each day in prayer. The more you practice it, the better you will get at it. Imagine how different your outlook on life would be if you had more faith. Imagine how differently you would respond to difficulties, temptations and even good things too. In other words, by increasing your faith daily you will build on it and learn to persevere when trials come.

My prayer for you
Lord Jesus, increase our faith as we learn to depend on you and trust you more

and more. Help us to crave your word: to read it, to heed it, and to test it, so it can truly become part of our lives. Lord, we desperately need more of you and less of ourselves. Thank you for your faithfulness in always keeping your word.

A TIME OF FASTING AND PRAYER

Matt. 5:6 (KJV)
Blessed [are] they which do hunger and thirst after righteousness: for they shall be filled.

Every year, beginning in the month of January is our annual consecration. For 21 days we are fasting and praying for ourselves, loved ones and the nation. The first 7 days is without food and the remaining 14 is what we call the 'Daniel's Fast' – one meal a day with no meat or sweets. It is both wonderful and mysterious. Fasting is abstaining from food to focus on a period of spiritual growth. Believers throughout the ages have gone without food to receive the word of God. Although there are several reasons to fast, here are 4 reasons that I have learned and want to share with you about fasting.

Although I believe there are many reasons for fasting I have chosen just 3 to share with you today.

1. Fasting is for spiritual breakthrough. We seek spiritual breakthrough, ask for mercy over our nation as well as our personal circumstances, and hunger for deeper revelation of God and His Word. Fasting speeds the release of God's promises by taking away distractions so, we can enter into His presence more easily.

2. Fasting is for direction. When we eliminate food from our diet for a number of days our spirit becomes uncluttered and sensitive to the things of God. It clarifies our desires and shows us the one thing that we can't live without.

3. Fasting will strengthen our prayer life. When we fast we are increasing the amount of time

available to pray, therefore drawing nearer to God. It gives you a newfound strength and dependence on Him.

There are a variety of benefits to fasting including the elimination of toxins that build up in your body.

Fasting is not a way to get God to do what we want. Fasting changes us and not God.

Fasting is done in a spirit of humility and joyfulness.

More reasons why we fast:

Are you in need of healing or a miracle?
Do you need the tender touch of God in your life?
Is there a dream inside you that only He can make possible?
Are you in need of a fresh encounter?
Do you desire a deeper, more intimate and powerful relationship with the Lord?
Are you ready to have heightened sensitivity to the desires of God?
Do you need to break away from bondages that have been holding you hostage?
Is there a friend or loved one that needs Salvation?
Do you desire to know God's will for your life?

DIARY OF A FAST

To help you understand what fasting, in conjunction with prayer, can do for you I have included below a diary of my fast this January.

Day 1

Today is the first day of my fast. I have mixed emotions. I am excited, anticipating what God is going to do for the next seven days. At the same time I am feeling somewhat overwhelmed. Seven days without food is a long time. Overall, my energy level is steady and I am feeling good.

> TODAY'S PRAYER:
> May my light break forth like the morning, my healing spring forth speedily and my righteousness go before me; May the glory of the Lord be my rear guard. When I call, may the Lord answer and when I cry, may He say, "Here I am" Isa. 58:8,9 (NHEB).

Day 2

This is the second day of my Fast. I am enjoying the time of prayer and worship. Today during worship service many shared their testimony of how God had healed their bodies. Excitement and anticipation is in the air.

> Matt. 6:33 (KJV)
> But seek ye first the Kingdom of God and his righteousness and all these things shall be added unto you.

Day 3

This is day number three of my fast. Today, the presence of the Lord met us in the prayer service. We were all strengthened and encouraged during noon day prayer. Each day I feel my body getting stronger and stronger.

My challenge for you today:
Focus on recognizing His presence in your daily routine. Look for ways that God is working in your relationships. Pray that He will show you ways that you can join His work and be a blessing to the people you encounter

Day 4

This is day four of my fast. The hunger pains and headaches that I experienced on the first and second days are gone. My water intake is very important during this time because my body is eliminating toxins and the water helps flush them out.

TODAY'S PRAYER:
Jesus, I know that growing closer to you will require more than giving up meals. I want to give you my time, my attention and all of my heart as I seek to know You more. Search my heart, Lord, and show me the things that are taking priority over You in my life.

Day 5

I have officially entered the fifth day of my fast. I have found a new strength. Although, I do not sleep long hours while on the fast, I do not feel weak or tired.

> Today's Prayer Isa.40:31 (KJV)
> But they that wait upon the Lord shall renew their strength; they shall mount up with wings as eagles; they shall run and not be weary; and they shall walk, and not faint.

Day 6

I am thankful for this fast. Today, it revealed some things in me that I had to release; I decided to let go of those things that burden and, or weigh me down.

> My Prayer for today
> God, clear my thoughts, my mind and my heart of all worry, fear and doubts.

Day 7

Today marks the end of the first week of my water fast! It's pretty amazing how quickly it just went by. This break from food has allowed me to think about my relationship with food and what to do about it. For sure, the fast has changed my perception on how much one actually needs food to survive. For the next fourteen days I will be on the Daniel Fast, no meats, no sweets and one meal a day.

Overall, I've become more conscious. This fast has definitely made me more grounded and calmer. I have learned several things during this fast. But the one thing that really stands out for me is my relationship with others. During the fast I decided to keep all my normal appointments and meetings with people. As I sat and listened each day (morning, noon and evening), I have learned that listening is an art and sometimes people are just wanting us to listen.

Thank you God for showing me to be more patient and understanding with people.

> Philippians 4:7 (KJV)
> And the peace of God, which passeth all understanding, shall keep your hearts and minds through Christ Jesus."

AND FINALLY....

I hope you have enjoyed reading this book and that it has shown you how the power of prayer can help you through the troubles and trials that make up the process of your journey through life, and to strengthen your faith in God.

If you'd like to read more about my work or to subscribe to updates on my blog just log on to http://www.mariareems.com and you'll find me there.

There are also two prayer CDs available to purchase which can be found at

http://www.mariareems.com/shop

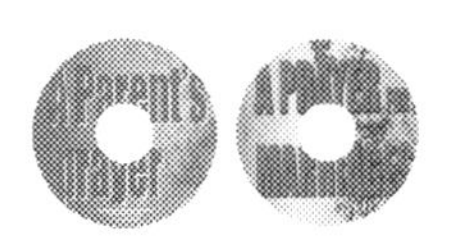

God bless you

Printed in the United States
By Bookmasters